BIRMINGHAM ON OLD POSTCARDS

(Volume Three)

John Marks

1. Corporation Street from Stephenson Place. The exchange building on the right has been demolished, but the view is still recognisable. Postcard published by Adams & Co., 48 Bristol Street, Birmingham.

£4.50

**Designed and Published by
Reflections of a Bygone Age,
Keyworth, Nottingham.
1990**

**Printed by
Adlard Print and Typesetting Services,
Ruddington, Notts.**

2. The Stork Hotel on the corner of Heathfield Road and Finch Road, selling Butler's Wolverhampton Ales. T. Bush was the licensee when this card was published about 1910.

Cover pictures:

Front: The Bull Ring, with Nelson and the Parish Church of St. Martins. The majority of local people remember the area with affection and greatly regret its redevelopment. Card by Valentine's of Dundee.

Back:
(top left) Wolseley motor car company advertising postcard, published by Davidson Bros. Comic design by Tom Browne.
(top right) Jevons & Mellor, Birmingham, advert card for Beehive knitting wools.
(bottom) Superb advertising card for the *Birmingham Gazette* and *Evening Despatch*.

ISBN 0 946245 30 4

BOURNVILLE WORKS.

3. Bournville works — a Cadbury's advertising card — an artistic, not photographic, design, and presumably published by the firm itself.

INDEX

INTRODUCTION

Picture Postcards were an extremely popular and important method of communication in the first two decades of this century. First introduced in Britain in 1894, they really took off when the Post Office allowed the message and address to occupy the same side of the card in 1902, enabling postcard publishers to use the whole of the other side for a picture.

Many local firms in Birmingham became specialists in view cards, and their combined output provides a marvellous record of the city and suburbs, especially in the 1900-14 period. Street scenes and events, many animated by the inclusion of people and transport, represent accurate pictures of the past, frozen at a particular time by the camera; messages on the back often complement and enhance the photographs.

Some of the best Birmingham publishers — Scott Russell, Harold Bott, Thomas Lewis, Adams & Co., and George E. Lewis — were profiled in the first two volumes, together with brief comments about others. Where the publisher of a postcard is known, this is mentioned in the captions, but many cards in fact were produced by anonymous firms or individuals. Postcard collectors find city centre views by the big national publishers like Valentine and Photocrom easiest to find, because these were produced in huge quantities. On the other hand, suburban street scenes can be quite elusive as they were normally printed in more limited numbers to reflect likely demand.

The postcard fulfilled several functions: it was a medium for communicating simple messages and greetings (mail was reliably delivered within 24 hours, and, over short distances, on the same day). Pictures of local scenes and events could be sent to friends and relatives to keep them up to date with goings-on. Firms used them as advertising cards — there are many good examples in this book.

Comic postcards gave people the opportunity to send risqué messages to their friends. Soon, the collecting of all these cards became a major hobby, and the reign of Edward VII paralleled the 'golden age' of Picture Postcards, with many thousands of families amassing vast numbers sent from all over Britain (and, for those with wealthy connections, the Continent). Specialist magazines catered for the craze, and publishers produced cards on all kinds of themes: railways, actresses, military, shipping, glamour, children, heraldic, royalty, political — as well as greetings, comic cards and street scenes. The Great War saw new themes developed — patriotic, political satire, and beautiful silk cards, embroidered in France, and sent home by British tommies to be lovingly treasured. Postcard collecting ceased to have the same meaning and appeal after the war, though. The quality of production deteriorated (some of the best pre-1914 cards had been printed in Germany), the postage rate doubled, and the national mood and social conditions had changed out of all recognition: it was a new era, with changed values and priorities. 'Golden Age' postcards lay neglected in their albums in attics for years, until a few enthusiasts in the 1950's ushered in a new-found appreciation for the beautiful old cards to a whole new generation. Their availability, though, remained confined to the shelves of occasional book and antique shops, and new-wave collectors didn't find it easy to build up collections. All that changed in the 1970's. A travelling exhibition organised by the Victoria and Albert Museum, the emergence of specialist dealers, magazines, catalogues and fairs, had the effect of encouraging a host of new collectors and a consequent upsurge in prices. By then, Edwardian albums were emerging from the attics, as their original owners or their sons and daughters died. Now, the hobby is thriving, and the beautiful postcard issues of the Edwardian era are once again lovingly collected.

CITY CENTRE

4. New Paradise Circus. This photographic postcard published by C. Richter of London is taken from the Hall of Remembrance in Broad Street, and shows the corner of Easy Row and Edmund Street.
The card was published in the fifties, before demolition for the Ringway and Library complex.

63970   BIRMINGHAM. EASY ROW

Paradise Street, Birmingham   Valentines Series

5. Paradise Street, with Christ Church (demolished in 1899) in the background. The buildings subsequently erected on the site, Galloways Corner, were themselves demolished in 1970. Card published by Valentine's of Dundee about 1903 from an earlier photograph.

6. The Post Office was opened in 1874 in Victoria Square. Card by unidentified publisher.

POST OFFICE, BIRMINGHAM.

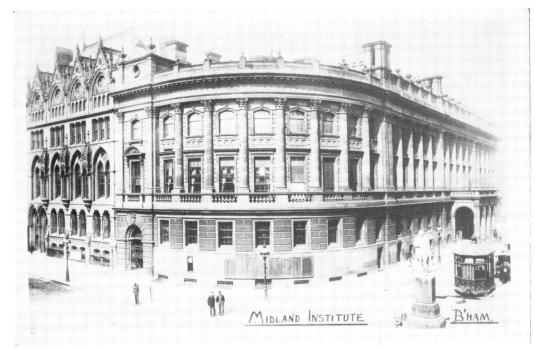

7. The Birmingham and Midland Institute was built in 1857 and demolished in 1965. Photographic card by Thomas Lewis of Stratford Road, Birmingham.

MIDLAND INSTITUTE B'HAM.

8. The Central Lending and Reference Library was an extension of the Midland Institute Building, and survived until 1974. This postcard, published by Wrench (no. 11409) was actually posted in Brighton in April 1905.

9. Postcard by J. Welch & Sons of Portsmouth (JWS 1432), featuring the circular reading room of the Reference Library.

Public Library & Reading Room, Birmingham.

ISLINGTON ROW. BIRMINGHAM.

10. Islington Row (now part of Middleway) on a card by Lilywhite of Halifax (no. 354 A) published in the 1920's.

BIRMINGHAM, ASTON STREET

11. Aston Street, like Islington Row on card 10, is now unrecognisable, with the buildings demolished, the area redeveloped, and the road filled to capacity with speeding traffic. This card was published by C. Richter.

NEW STREET, BIRMINGHAM,

10090-12

ROTARY PHOTO, E.C

12. New Street, with Worcester Street on the left, on a postcard by Rotary Photo Co. of London, posted in Birmingham in September 1913. King Edward's Grammar School is on the centre left.

13. King Edward VI school was rebuilt 1833-7 and demolished in 1936. It's seen here on a 1920's postcard by J. Willoughby Harrison of Small Heath.

KING EDWARD'S SCHOOL. NEW STREET. BIRMINGHAM.

14. New Street, with Worcester Street on the left and High Street on the right. Wrench series card, postally used in June 1908.

Birmingham. *New Street.*

The Wrench Series, No. 5781

15. View of High Street in the 1930's by Photocrom of Tunbridge Wells.

16. Bull Street from Dale End on a Scott Russell & Co. card, no. 290.

17. Corporation Street from the junction with New Street, on a photographic postcard by Timothy Jones & Co., Birmingham, posted from the city in April 1913.

18. Lewis's opened in 1886. A number of adjacent shops were added, and rebuilding took place up to 1928. No publisher indicated on the postcard.

19. A card by Valentine's of Corporation Street from the Old Square. On the right is the Grand Theatre of Varieties.

20. Digbeth Institute was founded by the Rev. J.H. Jowett M.A. in 1908, and shown in all its glory here on a card by Adams & Co.

FIRE STATION OVERLOOKING LANCASTER PLACE. BIRMINGHAM.

21. Lancaster Place, now Lancaster Circus, Queensway. A 1940's view by C. Richter of London.

22. The Great Western Hotel was built in 1863 and demolished in 1970. The cable tram ran from Colmore Row to Hockley Brook, later extended to New Inns. Postcard by Hugo Lang of Liverpool.

23. Colmore Row in 1906.

24. Superb Edwardian period photographic card by W.H. Day featuring Dudley Road and the corner of Moilliett Road, with Charles Shotton's pawnbrokers on the right.

25. The band of H.M. Scots Guards playing in Summerfield Park, on a postcard by Frank Nightingale of Smethwick.

26. Hagley Road in the early years of this century (the card was actually posted from Birmingham in 1906) showing two horse-buses.

27. Horse-buses were phased out gradually after the introduction of motor buses in 1903. Both can be seen on this c.1906 postcard.

28. After experiments with steam, cable and batteries, the electric tram reigned for fifty years until the last one ran in 1953. This postcard was postally used in July 1924, and together with the two above illustrates perfectly the development of public transport from the city centre to the suburbs.

29. Varna Road in 1910. It developed an unsavoury reputation after the second world war, but was redeveloped and is now known as Hay Park and Belgravia Close. Unidentified publisher, but the card was posted from Edgbaston in August 1910, with the message *"This is a street in the small village of Edgbaston. There are two houses of historical note, both of which are visible."*

30. A postcard by A.T. Ryberg of Edgbaston Street, posted from Birmingham in September 1913, and showing Coventry Road. In the middle distance is the junction with Charles Road.

31. Six Ways, Golden Hillock Road, on a card in the "Anderton" series, postally used in 1943. Note the Shell Motor Spirit tanker. This location is now the residence of a large flock of pigeons.

32. Churchill Road, Bordesley Green. The Era Picture Playhouse can be seen on the corner, with 'Flying Colours' the presentation. Postcard no. 12A in the 'Adco' series, posted in August 1919.

BALSALL HEATH

33. Moseley Road from the junction with Brighton Road.

34. Moseley Road – the baths and library are on the left.

35. The junction of Mary Street and Strensham Road. This photographic card, like the other two on this page, bears no publisher's name.

36. Hampton Court Road, on a postcard by George Lewis of Dudley Street, Birmingham. Shops featured are Stanley & Co. (cash drapers) at no. 4, Alex McNab (fish and poultry dealer), Cooper's Supply Stores, and A.G. Parsons. The card is of c.1910 vintage.

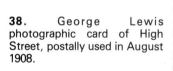

37. Old Cottages on Metchley Lane, on a postcard by Bradshaw of High Street, Harborne, posted from there in August 1925.

38. George Lewis photographic card of High Street, postally used in August 1908.

39. The corner of Albany Road and High Street, with Lloyds Bank prominent but little traffic on this 1911 George Lewis postcard. *"Got through it all right. Will give you a full description when I write on Friday"*, wrote the sender.

40. High Street from the junction with Vivian Road, and a horse-bus centre stage. Card posted from Birmingham in October 1904.

41. Postcard by Stanford & Mann, Harborne, used in September 1910 (posted at 8.15 p.m. from Harborne and addressed to Stratton House, Smethwick), with the message *"will call tomorrow Wed about 11.30. Hope it will be convenient."*

42. High Street, Saltley, with the "Adderley Arms" public house on the left. Posted in March 1910 to Dartford, enquiring *"Have you been to the Dartford rink yet and got the craze?"*

43. The junction of Alum Rock Road and Pelham Road, on a photographic card in 'Heighway's series' of Alum Rock Road. Posted at Birmingham in July 1929.

44. The Bridge, Saltley. Card by S.J. Swingler, Saltley Post Office, which was situated on the corner of Metropolitan Road and High Street, adjoining the "Adderley Arms" featured in card 42.

45. Couchman Road and the junction with College Road, with branch no. 20 of the Birmingham Industrial Co-op on the corner. Card posted in November 1911: *"I would like to exchange with you very much. I do not mind what sort of P.C.s"*. The writer lived in the far distance on this card.

46. The Wolseley factory on Drews Lane, showing staff leaving work.

47. Rural Saltley in 1918, showing Burney Lane, Alum Rock Road.

48. The junction of Bloomsbury Street (left) and Great Francis Street (right), with the "Junction Inn" centre and tramlines clearly visible.

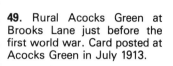

49. Rural Acocks Green at Brooks Lane just before the first world war. Card posted at Acocks Green in July 1913.

50. Fox Hollies Road, near the junction with Westfield Road. *"This is a lovely place – staying just near here",* wrote Mary to Miss Meadowcroft at Stockport in June 1917.

51. Stockfield Road, Acocks Green, in about 1910.

Three views of Warwick Road.
52. On the left is the junction with Oxford Road …

53. … and then the road drops towards Lincoln Road.

54. Photographic postcard by Geo. Lewis, postally used in June 1909.

55. Six Ways, Aston, at 2.30 p.m. on a sunny afternoon in an Edwardian summer. The tram advertises the Grand Theatre of Varieties, then in Corporation Street. Plenty of bicycles in evidence here!

56. The Home and Colonial Stores, 102 High Street, Aston – then one of sixteen branches in Birmingham. Long gone are the days when a small shop could boast of a manager and six staff! Perfect Margarine (Wholesome and Appetising) is advertised at 1/- on this c.1920 postcard.

57. Trinity Road in 1910, when you could safely walk in the middle of the street!

BOURNVILLE

58. In the early days at Cadbury's, women were provided with separate facilities of all kinds. This card by Scott Russell & Co. shows 'Bournville girls leaving cycle house'.

59. Box-filling in the works. Another Scott Russell card.

60. The so-called 'Rest House' on the village green was erected to commemorate the silver wedding of Mr. & Mrs. George Cadbury. This card shows the 'opening and presentation' on April 18th, 1914.

61. Many picture postcards were neither interesting nor beautiful. This card by Lilywhite of Halifax would seem to be a good example!

62. High Street, with the junction of Orphanage and Mason Roads in the distance. J.F. Darrall (butchers) and Henry Lett (grocer) are on the corner.

63. Mrs. M.W. Coulborn at 120 High Street was a china and glass dealer with a second shop at 44 Station Road. Postcard by Lilywhite.

HIGH STREET, ERDINGTON

64. A similar photograph taken a little further back. Edward Allsopp, coal and coke merchant, is on the right, and the 'Roe Buck Inn' in the middle distance.

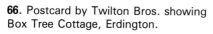

SIX WAYS. ERDINGTON.

65. Gravelly Hill, leading into High Street, Erdington, at Six Ways. Summer Road is on the left. The "Queen's Head" (licensee A.E. Butler) is on the left, with Erdington Taxi Garage and Archer's Supply Stores at the junction. Postcard by Adco, sent from Birmingham in June 1914.

66. Postcard by Twilton Bros. showing Box Tree Cottage, Erdington.

67. Mason Road, Erdington, in Dudley's Series postcard, pro-bably early in the 1920's. Featured in this row of shops are Alice Mayhew, hardware dealer, at no. 61, and Harry Dudley, confectioner, at 63.

SCHOOL ROAD, HALL GREEN   J.G.H., B.

68. The junction of School Road and Brooklands Road, on a postcard published by Boltons Library at Hall Green.

BALDWINS LANE HALL GREEN

Terminus nr. Shirley, Stratford Road, Hall Green.

69. Rural Hall Green, showing Baldwin's Lane in 1911.

70. The tram terminus – the service was extended to the city boundary in 1928, and this postcard dates from the following decade.

NEW BRIDGE STRATFORD RD B'M
HALL GREEN & SPRINGFIELD

71. The first bridge on this site at Stratford Road was built in 1715. This 'New' bridge was actually opened in 1913, and the illustrated card was posted on 6th August 1914, just after the outbreak of war. *"Things are in a dreadful state owing to the war"*, wrote R.Y. in a message to a relative in Cornwall. *"Food is an awful price and people (are) striving to buy as much as possible."*

HANDSWORTH

72. Lozells Road and Berners Street. F.W. Greenway is the draper's shop on the corner. Postcard published c.1910.

LOZELLS ROAD, FROM LOZELLS ST., LOOKING WEST, BIRMINGHAM.

73. The junction of Lozells Road and Lozells Street, on a postcard by Lilywhite. Next to J. Scott & Co. (modern house furnishers) on the right is the Post Office. This card was posted at Kidderminster in June 1924.

74. Soho Hill and Hamstead Road.

HEATHFIELD ROAD, HANDSWORTH.

75. Postcard by Leonard, Smith & Co. of Cannon Street in the 'Lens' series no. 501, posted from Birmingham in September 1905. Heathfield Road is the featured location.

76. Soho Road in the late 1930's on a Valentine's postcard.

SOHO ROAD, HANDSWORTH.   G.7947.

77. Another card by the same publisher, posted in July 1936. New Inns, Handsworth, with 'The Albion Picture Theatre' on the left.

G.207.   NEW INNS, HANDSWORTH. (39)

KINGS HEATH

78. High Street, opposite Vicarage Road, on a postcard mailed in April 1910 from King's Heath. Middleton & Jones (builders' merchants) and John Genders (painter and decorator) occupy the two premises on the right of the picture.

79. Though the roads remain, it is difficult to imagine this tranquil scene when viewing today's traffic nightmare at the junction of All Saints Road and Vicarage Road. Card posted in September 1912.

80. Vicarage Road, with Abbots Road on the right, on a 1912 postcard.

KINGS NORTON

81. The Green early this century on a postcard by A.T. Ryberg, posted from Kings Heath in August 1915.

82. The top of Parsons Hill and Walkers Heath Road (now sealed off at this point) from Broad Meadow Lane.

83. Walkers Heath Road, now developed beyond recognition. This postcard was sent in July 1912.

84. Kings Norton looking from the Green down Wharf Road. Postcard by Lilywhite (no. 216 A), posted in August 1914.

KINGS NORTON VILLAGE. BIRMINGHAM.   216 A

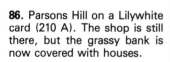

85. Lifford Lane, still a lane but with industrial development on both sides. This card was published in 1915.

86. Parsons Hill on a Lilywhite card (210 A). The shop is still there, but the grassy bank is now covered with houses.

PARSONS HILL. KINGS NORTON   210 A

87. Photographic postcard captioned 'Moseley Village', published about 1906. It shows Alcester Road, with King Edward's Place on the right.

88. Woodbridge Road, with the Trafalgar Road junction on the right. As in the above picture, the main features of this scene are still the same today. Postally used in August 1913.

89. Park Garage, near the junction of Alcester and Chantry Roads.

90. St. Mary's Row, looking down to Alcester Road, with St. Mary's Church to the right. Postcard by G.E. Lewis, posted in September 1911.

91. Somewhere in Wake Green Road, before the area was fully developed. Anonymously-published photographic postcard.

92. Belle Walk from Wake Green Road, in the grip of a very heavy frost. A bobby on the beat has obviously been enrolled by the photographer to enliven the scene.

93. Bristol Road, on a card posted at Edgbaston in August 1911. The junction with Rochester Road (seen more clearly in the following view) is approximately halfway down on the right.

94. Bristol Road from the corner of Rochester Road.

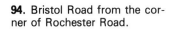

95. Church Hill, Northfield, photographed from the railway bridge seen on the next card. This one was postally used in September 1918.

96. West Heath Road looking towards the railway. Station Road is on the left. Card sent to Pocklington in October 1910.

97. The Old Toll House, on Bristol Road at Northfield.

98. Merritts Brook Lane, Northfield, on a card published by Lambson of the village, and posted in August 1937.

Merritts Brook Lane, Northfield.

99. Bristol Road – a view taken from its junction with Oak Tree Lane. The Ten Acres and Stirchley Co-op branch on the corner was opened in 1910.

100. The old Oak of Oak Tree Lane was felled in 1909, but not before it had been captured on a Scott Russell postcard.

101. The "New Inn" became "The Plough and Harrow" in 1904. This postcard must have been published shortly after its renaming, because it was posted in July 1905.

102. Bournbrook High Street on a c.1910 postcard.

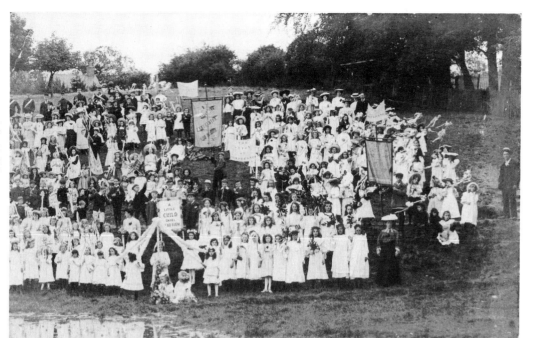

103. Massive children's gathering at a Band of Hope/Temperance movement demonstration. Photographic postcard by Compton of Bournbrook.

104. Birmingham 'Win the War' day was on 21st September 1918. This wagon was the contribution of Decimals Ltd. of Grange Road, Selly Oak, who are displaying "signal & phosphorus grenades" and "barbed wire cutters".

105. The People's Hall on Oak Tree Lane was built in 1910. On this c.1913 postcard it features as a 'Picturedrome', with twice-nightly shows. *"I thought you would like this one for your album"*, runs the message.

106. J.J. Snell's well-stocked hosiery shop at 738 Stratford Road, Sparkbrook.

107. The Mirror Laundry on Formans Road, situated between Perry Road and the river. The reverse of this postcard was used as a correspondence card for customers wishing to give orders.

108. Taylor Memorial Home at 142-4 Showell Green Lane. Later it became the 'Home from Home for Girls' (1942) and the women's hospital out-patients department (1947).

109. Stratford Road from the junction with Erasmus Road. A steam tram is in the middle distance on this postcard by Valentine of Dundee.

110. Postcard by Thomas Lewis of Farm Road from Stratford Road, published about 1911.

FARM ROAD. 1143.

PALMERSTON RD. SPARKBROOK

111. Palmerston Road, Sparkbrook, with Conway Road school in the distance.

112. Stratford Road, Sparkhill, with the 'Metropolitan Bank of England and Wales' on the right. This is a little way before the junction with Warwick Road. Card published by Geo. E. Lewis and posted on 14th August 1914. May Smith wrote to Miss A. Withers: *"Make the most of the last few days ... isn't the war dreadful? It has upset things terribly."*

STRATFORD ROAD, SPARKHILL.

Before extensive improvements to the course of the River Rea, Stirchley and Dogpool were subject to annual flooding. Seen here are

113. Pershore Road, 1st June 1924.

114. The bottom of Cartland Road, 1st June 1924.

115. Pershore Road, 11th July 1927.

116. Pershore Road and St. Stephens Road, 11th July 1927.

YARDLEY

117. Yew Tree Lane on a postcard published by E. Manley, Hay Mills Studio, Coventry Road, Hay Mills.

118. The ford at Hob Moor Road – the River Cole crossing near Haybarn recreation ground. 1920's wintry scene.

119. The development of the suburban lanes into housing estates took place in the twenties and thirties, with this view of Barrows Lane at Yardley an excellent photographic example of the trend.

YARDLEY WOOD

120. Priory Road, with the mill pond on the left. Postcard sent from Kings Heath in December 1913. *"This is a lovely spot in summer."*

121. A card by Geo. E. Lewis of Slade Lane with the River Cole in the distance. The photograph was taken from the Priory Road end.

122. Yardley Wood Post Office, also described over the window as Warstock Post Office, on a c.1912 postcard.

PERRY BARR

123. Aldridge Road, Perry Barr, on a postcard published by Frank Nightingale (no. 525) and posted in September 1908. *"We are having dreadful weather here"*, was part of the message.

124. The Boars Head Inn, Perry Barr, on a card posted from Birmingham in September 1912.

125. Walsall Road, Perry Barr, on a Geo. Lewis card.

126. This postcard of Rockey Lane was used in September 1908.

127. Midland View Co. (Birmingham) postcard of the "Fox and Goose Hotel", advertising 'Home Brewing' and 'Good Stabling'.

128. Albert Road, Stechford, photographed by Geo. E. Lewis in 1909.

129. Flaxley Lane, later upgraded to the status of Road with the expansion of building. The shop on the right was on the corner of Iron Lane.

SUTTON COLDFIELD

130. The Council House and Town Hall, opened in 1906. Station Street is on the left.

131. The last of Sutton's thirteen watermills. New Hall Mill was built nearly 300 years ago to grind flour.

132. The original Moor Hall was demolished in 1903 and a new house built in 1905, the home of Colonel Ansell. Card posted from Sutton Coldfield in September 1912.

133. Mrs. Ansell's car and chauffeur. The postcard was sent from Moor Hall by a Mrs. Holmes.

TRANSE

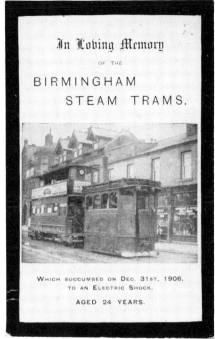

CABLE CAR'S FAREWELL.

Farewell, kind friends, I'm going
To the scrap heap, so they say;
The worthy City Fathers
Think too long I've had the sway.
They deem me old and ugly,
In fact, not up to date;
If ever love they had for me
Their love's turned into hate.

This city's known as "Forward"—
A motto that means well;
'Tis that what makes them anxious
The cable car to sell.
Some say that I'm not handsome,
But most of them agree
When electric cars they take my place
Improvement there will be.

And now before I leave you
Kind friends take my advice;
And you, both guards and drivers
Who all have acted nice
Give our a hearty welcome
When the new friend does appear;
For though his name's Electric Car
To your welfare he's sincere.

Composed by John Bryan.

134. Cable Cars were introduced in 1887. The last one ran in 1911. This card features a valedictory poem by John Bryan.

135. One of many 'In Memoriam' cards issued to commemorate the end of over twenty years of steam trams.

136. Open-top United Electric Car introduced between 1905-8, and fitted with a top during the war. This postcard features a scene on Pershore Road opposite Elm Tree Road.

137. Cable car in Colmore Row on a postcard by Knight Brothers.

138. Car no. 27, built 1905-8, in Dudley Road near the junction with Heath Green Lane. Postcard by Nightingale.

139. A happy memory of weekend outings for many Birmingham people. The terminus at Rednal, shown on a postcard by B.J. Baker of Rednal Post Office.

REDNAL, THE TRAM TERMINUS

TRAM TERMINUS, ERDINGTON.

140. Car 634 at Erdington tram terminus. Originally an open-topped car, it was fitted with a top between 1927-31. The card was posted at Haselor in June 1924.

141. Oxhill Road, Handsworth, showing the tram terminus adjacent to Stockwell Road. Card by Adco of Bristol Street (no. 601).

OXHILL ROAD, HANDSWORTH No 601.   COPYRIGHT A

RAILWAY STATIONS

NEW ST., (L.M.S.) STATION, BIRMINGHAM.

142. Postcard by J. Willoughby Harrison of Small Heath posted from Moseley in August 1932. Lots of interest in this view of New Street station from above.

SNOW HILL STATION, BIRMINGHAM.

143. Snow Hill, seen here on a postcard in the "City" series, was opened in 1852.

144. Gravelly Hill station on the Sutton Coldfield Railway, an offshoot of the London and North Western. Postcard by R. Benton of Erdington.

145. Kings Norton station was opened in 1849, nine years after the L.M.S. line to Gloucester was built. In 1871, the Birmingham West Suburban Railway was authorised to run from Granville Street to a junction at Kings Norton.

146. Acocks Green on the Oxford Junction Railway — later part of the Great Western. The original station was completed in 1852, and this photographic postcard (sent from Birmingham in December 1909) shows it in 1909 after rebuilding. Compare the view in vol.1 (illus. 199).

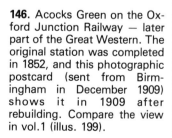

HORSE TRANSPORT

147. Photographic postcard identified on the reverse as *'107 Rotton Park, Edgbaston: Bobby and Dot off to school'.*

148. Dartmouth Street, Birmingham, featuring a line of cabs, including one on the left owned by B. Thorpe of 86 Baker Street.

149. Part of a parade in Constitution Hill. Newbury's were the predecessors of Lewis's.

MOTOR
TRANSPORT

150. No identification here, but it's a Birmingham-registered coach ready for a day trip.

151. An advertising card for the very latest 1930's coach design.

HIRE OUR RADIO SUNSHINE SALOON COACHES FOR YOUR SUMMER OUTINGS

DALTON'S GARAGE, Ltd., 272, Soho Road, Handsworth, BIRMINGHAM.

Telephone :   0457 Northern.

152. Two lorries owned by E. Wallin (Aston Model Sawing Company) of Upper Webster Street, Aston. Postcard by Purcell and Betts of Aston Road North.

153. The Austin Motor Co. Herbert Austin, wearing a bowler and carrying a cane, is seated in the centre; surrounding him are his North Works employees.

154. This photographic postcard, with March 1909 postal usage, bears the message *"I am working at the Austin"*. Herbert Austin's Longbridge factory was built on a derelict site after he purchased the land in November 1905.

155. This 1-ton steam Sentinel was owned by Mackie and Gladstone, wholesale wine and spirit merchants of Dale End.

156. Postcard by H. Munro of a day trip of Cadbury employees and their children in the 1920's, probably pictured near Edgbaston.

157. Card posted at Kings Heath in April 1907, showing the Stratford-on-Avon canal at Yardley Wood.

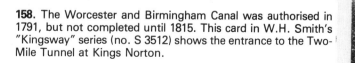

158. The Worcester and Birmingham Canal was authorised in 1791, but not completed until 1815. This card in W.H. Smith's "Kingsway" series (no. S 3512) shows the entrance to the Two-Mile Tunnel at Kings Norton.

S 3512   TWO MILE TUNNEL, KINGS NORTON

AMUSEMENTS

159. A maypole somewhere in Edgbaston in 1906.

160. Birmingham's Michaelmas Fair is first mentioned in 1400. Onions were the principal merchandise in the last century, hence its secondary name of Birmingham Onion Fair. It originally covered the whole of the centre of the town, but from 1861 was restricted to the Bull Ring. This view was taken in 1907 by an anonymous photographer. This century the Fair has steadily declined.

PICTURE HOUSES

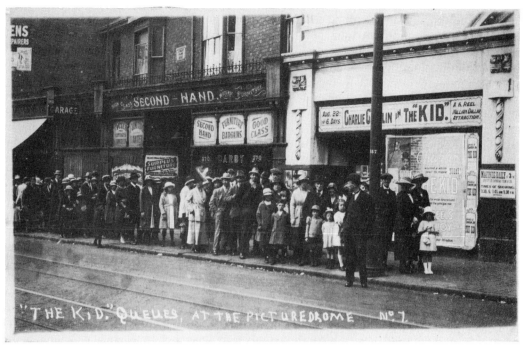

161. The Picturedrome at 372-6 Stratford Road. Opened in 1912, it was replaced by The Piccadilly in 1930. Charlie Chaplin in 'The Kid' was the attraction when Hubert Tolley of Ivor Road took this photograph.

162. The Picture House, Lozells, opened in 1911 and rebuilt in 1922. It was bombed during the second world war.

163. The Picturedrome at 287 Birchfield Road, Perry Barr, was opened about 1912. Charlie Chaplin's 'An Aviator's Love Affair' was showing when this photo was taken — probably just before the card was posted in March 1927.

164. The Beggars Bush, Chester Road, Erdington.

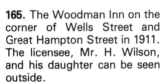

165. The Woodman Inn on the corner of Wells Street and Great Hampton Street in 1911. The licensee, Mr. H. Wilson, and his daughter can be seen outside.

166. 'Birmingham's Best Beer 1d' and 'Holt Championship Ale 1½d' are advertised at 84 Cambridge Street, Birmingham.

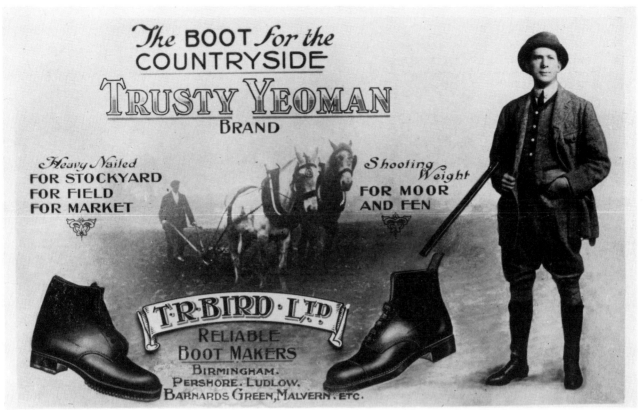

167. T.R. Bird, shoe and bootmakers, had branches in Worcestershire as well as Birmingham.

168. In the days before telephones took over our lives, most firms had their own advertising postcards, either for sending out short messages or acknowledgements, or for leaving with customers to return their orders on. This example is from Hammond Turner & Sons Ltd., and dates from the early 1920's.

169. H.C. Smith's textile warehouse published this 1917 advertising postcard.

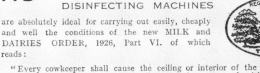

"FOUR OAKS"
MILK AND DAIRIES ORDER, 1926.

SPRAYING, LIMEWASHING AND DISINFECTING MACHINES

are absolutely ideal for carrying out easily, cheaply and well the conditions of the new MILK and DAIRIES ORDER, 1926, Part VI. of which reads:

"Every cowkeeper shall cause the ceiling or interior of the roof and the walls of every cowshed to be properly limewashed or sprayed with lime or otherwise disinfected twice at least in every year, once during April or May and once during September or October."

THIS ORDER CAME INTO FORCE OCT. 1ST AND THERE ARE HEAVY PENALTIES FOR NON-COMPLIANCE.

Illustration shows "WIZARD" *Pattern Limewashing a high wall. Price of this machine (capacity 6 galls.) and complete with 10-ft. rubber hose* £4 19s. 6d. *and 2 nozzles* ... ...

Other patterns: "Farmer" 62/6, "Farmer-de-Luxe" 68/-, "Dairyman" 80/-.

Catalogues FREE on application to the Sole Manufacturers

THE FOUR OAKS SPRAYING MACHINE CO.,
FOUR OAKS, SUTTON COLDFIELD, Nr. BIRMINGHAM.

Wire: "Sprayers, Four Oaks." 'Phone: 305 Sutton Coldfield.

Four Oaks Sprayers are not cheap toys, but good quality, practical machines, with 31 years' reputation behind them. ORIGINAL *and best.*

INSIST ON FOUR OAKS.

Prosecutions are already taking place for neglecting to carry out the provisions of this new order. Post this card to-day and avoid all risk.

170. Promotional card for the Four Oaks Spraying Machine Company, 1926. Reverse was used as a correspondence card.

171. Postcard issued by Saffell and Martin in 1931.

Sole Agents for "Triumph Auto" Pianos And Music Rolls — Easy Payments Arranged

SAFFELL & MARTIN LTD.

Gramophones
Radio-Gramophones
Records
Accessories
All-Electric
Radio
Tunings
Repairs
Exchanges

Piano & Player Piano Manufacturers:

118 DALE END (Bull Street Corner) BIRMINGHAM.

Telephone Central 1401. And at London, Cardiff and Dudley.

172. The Waterloo Bar and Restaurant, New Street, Birmingham, about 1912.

THE WATERLOO BAR, New Street, Birmingham.

G. W. HARDY, Proprietor. FREE HOUSE. Telephone 04550.

THEATRE ADVERTS

Most theatres and cinemas advertised their shows on postcards, the fronts being portraits of the stars, scenes from the play, or just views of the town.

173. Marie Tempest, appearing at the Prince of Wales Theatre in September 1909, actually wrote and signed this card herself. Both front and back shown.

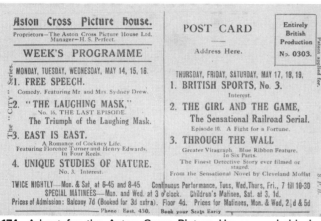

174. Advert for the Aston Cross Picture House, probably in 1918. A picture of Birmingham University is on the other side.

175. Design by Edwardian artist Dudley Hardy, who was responsible for many theatre posters and comic postcards, for "Aladdin" at the Grand Theatre.

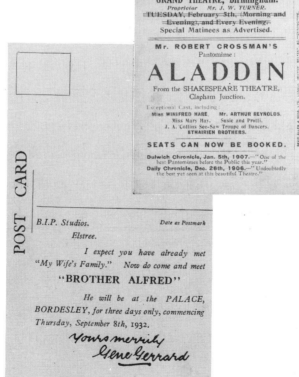

176. Gene Gerrard was appearing at the Palace, Bordesley, in September 1932.

177. Two Dennis motor tenders on display at the Central Fire Station in the Upper Priory, 1910. Postcard by Austin Bros., Bolton Road, Small Heath.

178. One of two 750-gallon steam fire engines on view in the Upper Priory at a special 'Past and Present' exhibition, 1910.

179. Another in Austin's 'Birmingham Fire Brigade' series – horse-drawn tender.

180. Burnt-out musical instrument workshop, possibly Gisborne's at 37 Suffolk Street. Postcard by F.S. Baker of Bristol Street.

181. Life-saving drill – another card in the Austin series.

182. Fire at Williams and Farmers' timber wharf on the canal side at Holiday Street in 1935. Many of the buildings visible on this postcard have long since gone.

183. Deep snow was a favourite subject for postcard publishers, as here at Station Road, Acocks Green, in January 1912, when Geo. Lewis photographed the scene for posterity.

184. Damage caused by a tornado crossing Small Heath on Sunday 14th June 1931. This view by Lacey's Studios of Coventry Road shows shops in Green Lane.

185. Three men were killed and windows were broken up to half a mile away when there was an explosion at Saltley Gas Works on Monday 10th October 1904.

186. Alf Messenger from Birmingham was a member of the British Olympic team in 1912 when he was photographed here by Purcell and Betts of Aston Road.

187. Birmingham boxer Arthur 'Boy' Edge.

188. Birmingham Police Cricket Club 1909, photographed by Ridge of Saltley.

189. Visit of Edward VII and Queen Alexandra to Birmingham on 7th July 1909.

190. The gas department's welcome arch for the same visit. See volume 1 (illus. 214-216) and volume 2 (illus. 145-149) for other cards of the event.